BIOGRAPHIES

BENJAMIN FRANKLIN

by Laura K. Murray

I0891791

PEBBLE
a capstone imprint

Pebble Explore is published by Pebble, an imprint of Capstone.
1710 Roe Crest Drive
North Mankato, Minnesota 56003
www.capstonepub.com

Copyright © 2021 by Capstone.
All rights reserved. No part of this publication may be reproduced in whole or in part, or stored in a retrieval system, or transmitted in any form or by any means, electronic, mechanical, photocopying, recording, or otherwise, without written permission of the publisher.

Library of Congress Cataloging-in-Publication Data is available on the Library of Congress website.
ISBN 978-1-9771-2330-5 (library binding)
ISBN 978-1-9771-2655-9 (paperback)
ISBN 978-1-9771-2338-1 (ebook pdf)

Summary: Describes the life of Benjamin Franklin, a Founding Father, author, and inventor. You'll learn about the early life, challenges, and major accomplishments of this important American.

Image Credits
Alamy: The Protected Art Archive, 17; Architect of the Capitol: 22; Getty Images: Bettmann, 7, 23, UIG/Universal History Archive, 19; iStockphoto: duncan1890, 13, ilbusca, 16; Library of Congress: 5, 10, 12, 20, 21, 29; The Metropolitan Museum of Art: The Friedsam Collection, Bequest of Michael Friedsam, 1931, cover, 1; The New York Public Library, 6, 9, 11, 27; North Wind Picture Archives: 15; Shutterstock: dnd_project, 26, Lee Snider Photo Images, 25, Olena Rodina (geometric background), cover, back cover, 2, 29

Editorial Credits
Editor: Erika L. Shores; Designer: Elyse White; Media Researcher: Svetlana Zhurkin; Production Specialist: Spencer Rosio

All internet sites appearing in back matter were available and accurate when this book was sent to press.

Printed in the United States 6554

Table of Contents

Who Was Benjamin Franklin? 4

Growing Up Benjamin 6

Ben the Printer 10

Big Ideas 14

Making America 18

Remembering Benjamin 24

Important Dates 28

Fast Facts 29

Glossary 30

Read More 31

Internet Sites 31

Index 32

Words in **bold** are in the glossary.

Who Was Benjamin Franklin?

Benjamin Franklin had big ideas. He helped make the country we know today. He was a leader in early America. Benjamin helped write and sign important papers for the United States. He also helped work with France and other countries.

Benjamin looked for ways to make life better. He started hospitals and schools. The new things he made, or invented, helped people. He was a scientist, **inventor**, and writer.

Growing Up Benjamin

Benjamin was born more than 300 years ago on January 17, 1706. His family lived in Boston, Massachusetts. At that time, America was made up of **colonies**. They were ruled by Great Britain.

Benjamin's birthplace in Boston

Young Benjamin (right) in his brother's print shop

As a boy, Benjamin wanted to sail on ships. He loved the sea. He also loved to learn. He read all the books he could.

Benjamin went to school from ages 8 to 10. Then he worked in his family's shop. They made soap and candles. At age 12, Benjamin went to work at his brother's print shop.

Benjamin learned about printing and writing. He wrote letters in the newspaper. But he did not want people to know he wrote them. He made up the name Silence Dogood.

Benjamin was not happy working at the print shop. His brother treated him badly. At age 17, Benjamin ran away to Philadelphia, Pennsylvania. He wanted to start life on his own.

Benjamin in Philadelphia

Ben the Printer

Benjamin worked hard. In 1728, at age 22, he opened a print shop. The next year, he bought a newspaper. It was called *The Pennsylvania Gazette*. Many people read the paper. Benjamin became rich.

Benjamin in his print shop

Deborah Read

As a young man, Benjamin met Deborah Read. She ran a store. They married in 1730. Benjamin already had a son named William. He and Deborah had two children together. They were named Francis and Sarah.

People borrowed books from the library Benjamin started in Philadelphia.

In the 1700s, many people could not pay for books. Benjamin wanted people to read and learn. In 1731, he helped start the first library in Philadelphia.

In 1732, Benjamin wrote *Poor Richard's Almanack*. This short book came out every year. It had a calendar, stories, and poems. It covered weather and farming too. Some of what Benjamin wrote became famous sayings. One of them was, "No gains without pains." People today say, "No pain, no gain."

The front cover of *Poor Richard's Almanack* in 1733

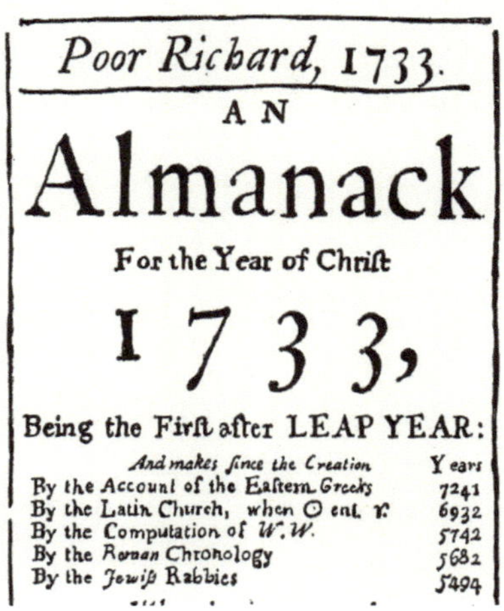
Poor Richard, 1733.
AN
Almanack
For the Year of Christ
1733,
Being the First after LEAP YEAR:

And makes since the Creation	Years
By the Account of the Eastern *Greeks*	7241
By the Latin Church, when ☉ ent. ♈	6932
By the Computation of *W. W.*	5742
By the *Roman* Chronology	5682
By the *Jewish* Rabbies	5494

Big Ideas

Many people knew Benjamin had big ideas. In 1751, he was chosen to work in Pennsylvania's **government**. He also started the University of Pennsylvania. During that time, he helped start the first hospital in America as well.

Benjamin liked to study science and weather. He did experiments. In 1752, he tied a metal key to a kite. He flew the kite during a storm. Benjamin touched the key on the string. There was a spark! He showed that lightning was electricity.

Benjamin flew a kite during a storm to study electricity.

Benjamin invented many things during his life. The Franklin stove heated homes safely. Bifocals helped people see near and far. The lightning rod kept buildings safe from lightning.

Benjamin loved to swim. He studied the oceans. He made swim fins to help him swim faster.

Lightning rods were placed on tall buildings.

Benjamin invented and played the armonica.

Benjamin liked music too. He invented the glass armonica. It used glass bowls to make different sounds. Benjamin also played the violin, harp, and guitar.

Making America

Benjamin and other leaders in the colonies were unhappy with British rule. They said British laws and taxes were unfair.

One unfair law was the Stamp Act of 1765. It made colonists pay a tax, or fee, on newspapers and other printed works. Benjamin spoke to British leaders. They ended the Stamp Act in 1766.

Benjamin met with British leaders.

Benjamin (left) helped write the Declaration of Independence.

At age 69, Benjamin was part of the Second **Continental Congress**. The group voted to break free from the British. During the **Revolutionary War** (1775–1783), the colonies fought to be a free country. In 1776, Benjamin helped write the **Declaration of Independence**. It told the British that the colonies were free.

In 1776, Benjamin moved to France. He served as the **ambassador** to France until 1785. He helped the United States and France become strong partners. Benjamin was also the ambassador to Sweden.

Benjamin in France

signing of the Constitution

The war with Great Britain lasted eight years. In 1783, Benjamin signed the Treaty of Paris. It ended the war. The United States was a free country! Two years later, Benjamin became **governor** of Pennsylvania. He led the state for three years.

In 1787, Benjamin helped write and sign the U.S. Constitution. The document set up the U.S. government.

Benjamin died on April 17, 1790. He was 84 years old. He was buried in Philadelphia. People around the world were sad to say goodbye.

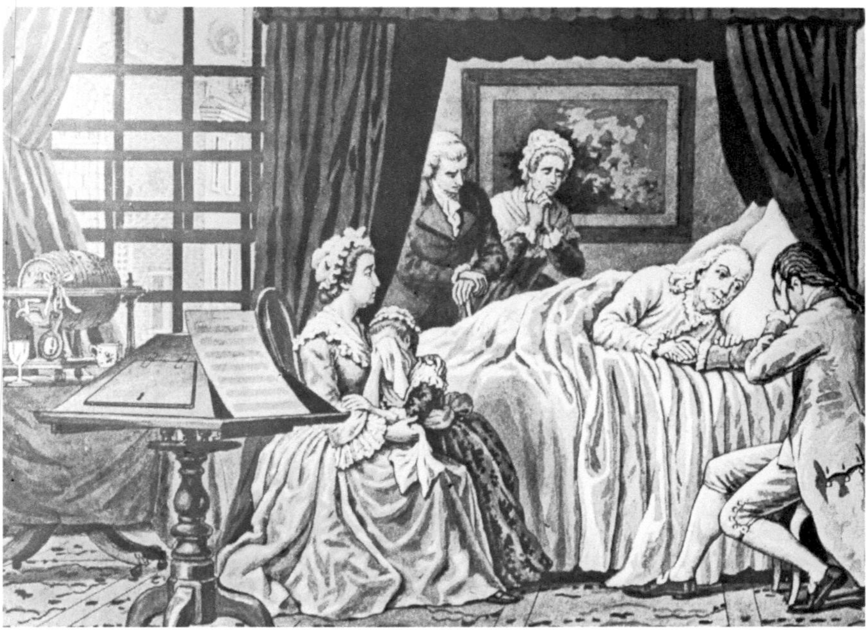

Remembering Benjamin

Today, people visit Philadelphia to learn about Benjamin's life. They go to a science museum named for him. The Benjamin Franklin National Memorial is inside. It has a large statue of Benjamin.

People also visit the Benjamin Franklin Museum in Philadelphia. It has items from Benjamin's life. Independence Hall stands nearby. It is where Benjamin and other leaders signed the Declaration of Independence.

Schools, museums, and other buildings are named for Benjamin. A **crater** on the moon is named for him too! Benjamin's face is on the $100 bill. The other side shows Independence Hall.

Benjamin Franklin was a great leader. He worked hard all his life. He asked questions about the world. He wanted people to read, learn, and work together. He knew that people could make the world a better place.

Important Dates

January 17, 1706	Benjamin Franklin is born in Boston.
1722	Benjamin writes his first letter as Silence Dogood.
September 1, 1730	Benjamin marries Deborah Read.
1732	Benjamin publishes the first *Poor Richard's Almanack*.
1751	Benjamin is elected to the Pennsylvania Assembly.
1752	Benjamin flies a kite during a lightning storm to study electricity.
1775	Benjamin is part of the Second Continental Congress.
1776	Benjamin signs the Declaration of Independence.
1776	Benjamin becomes first U.S. ambassador to France.
1783	Benjamin signs the Treaty of Paris.
1787	Benjamin signs the U.S. Constitution.
April 17, 1790	Benjamin dies in Philadelphia.

Fast Facts

Name:
Benjamin Franklin

Role:
writer, scientist, inventor, government leader

Life dates:
January 17, 1706 to April 17, 1790

Key accomplishments:
Benjamin Franklin helped create and signed the Declaration of Independence (1776), Treaty of Paris (1783), and U.S. Constitution (1787). He invented many things, including bifocals and the lightning rod.

Glossary

ambassador (am-BA-suh-duhr)—a person sent by a government to represent it in another country

colony (KAH-luh-nee)—an area that has been settled by people from another country and is owned by that country

Continental Congress (kahn-tuh-nen-tuhl KAHNG-gruhs)—leaders from the 13 original American colonies who made up the American government from 1774 to 1789

crater (KRAY-tuhr)—a hole made when large pieces of rock crash into a planet or moon's surface

Declaration of Independence (dek-luh-RAY-shuhn UV in-di-PEN-duhnss)—a document that declares the United States a free country

government (GUHV-urn-muhnt)—the group of people who make rules and decisions for a country or state

governor (GUHV-urn-ur)—the leader of a state

inventor (in-VENT-ur)—someone who thinks up and makes something new

Revolutionary War (rev-uh-LOO-shuhn-air-ee WOR)—the American colonies' fight from 1775 to 1783 for freedom from Great Britain

Read More

Dickmann, Nancy. *Benjamin Franklin: The Man Behind the Lightning Rod.* North Mankato, MN: Pebble, 2020.

Duling, Kaitlyn. *Benjamin Franklin: Inventor and Founding Father.* New York: Cavendish Square, 2020.

Schulman, Mark. *Benjamin Franklin: Inventor of the Nation!* San Diego, CA: Portable Press, 2020.

Internet Sites

The Franklin Institute: Benjamin Franklin
www.fi.edu/benjamin-franklin/resources

Time for Kids: Benjamin Franklin
www.timeforkids.com/g34/benjamin-franklin/

Index

ambassadors, 21, 28

Benjamin Franklin National Memorial, 24
birth, 6, 28, 29
books, 7, 12, 13

children, 11
colonies, 6, 18, 20

death, 23, 28, 29
Declaration of Independence, 20, 24, 28, 29

electricity, 14, 28
experiments, 14

family, 6, 7, 8, 11
famous sayings, 13

governors, 22
Great Britain, 6, 18, 20, 22

hospitals, 4, 14

Independence Hall, 24, 26
inventions, 4, 16, 17, 29

libraries, 12

museums, 24, 26

newspapers, 8, 10, 18

Philadelphia, Pennsylvania, 8, 12, 23, 24
Poor Richard's Almanack, 13, 28
printing, 7, 8, 10

Read, Deborah, 11, 28
Revolutionary War, 20, 22

schools, 4, 7, 26
Second Continental Congress, 20, 28
Stamp Act, 18

taxes, 18
Treaty of Paris, 22, 28, 29

University of Pennsylvania, 14
U.S. Constitution, 23, 28, 29